T0063945

THIS IS A GREAT MYSTERY

GOD'S RIGHTS

DONALD FRITH

authorHOUSE®

AuthorHouse™
1663 Liberty Drive
Bloomington, IN 47403
www.authorhouse.com
Phone: 1-800-839-8640

Scripture quotations marked KJV are from the Holy Bible, King James Version (Authorized Version). First published in 1611. Quoted from the KJV Classic Reference Bible, Copyright © 1983 by The Zondervan Corporation.

Published by AuthorHouse 09/05/2014

ISBN: 978-1-4969-3910-4 (sc)
ISBN: 978-1-4969-3909-8 (e)

CONTENTS

This book is a result of the Monday May 20, 2013 Moore, Oklahoma tornado where almost all things acquired from the world were blown away. The back end of a pickup truck hauled away me, my wife Becky, my two dogs in their crates (Simon and Hannah), two of our four cats (Madison and Mary), a few clothes, some medicines and breathing equipment, and a laptop.

The Thursday after, another of our cats was found in the remains of the master bedroom closet which we used as test shelter with the animals. Mulligan (the oldest male) hid in what he could find in the closet and waited for our return. Fond tears of joy were shed as he climbed into our arms and wanted to be held tightly.

After months of animal rescue groups looking night and day no sign of David, the youngest male and largest of the cats, was found. In to the hands of God he was given.

Sitting in the hallway between bedrooms we watched as the roof arose up and away, then the destruction of the ceilings, and then the walls. As a rafter from the roof rammed into the wall a foot in front of us, we knew that only God was in control. We watched objects in the room in front of us circle through the room. As we watched the sky above be covered with pieces of what the tornado devoured we gave the whole over to God, and we watched without fear and injury.

We walked over four feet of debris as we left the house. We walked to the curb to view the neighborhood. The houses around us were gone. We were in the center of that tornado, but God sent us out for a reason. Neighbors helped pull out the dog crates, the two cats, and what little we had. We left in the back of a gentleman's pickup truck. According to the emergency people the only way out was to walk, yet God sent a stranger with his truck.

With help from local people and local groups we received food and supplies. With help from people, churches, and groups from other states some items of value were found and saved, including Mulligan. Through our church we found comfort. Our vet cared for our pets until we were able to find a home. To all those who in their way supplied support this book is dedicated.

God left us most of our animals, but took David for Himself. God left our bodies and minds uninjured. God tore away all that we treasured and scattered it miles away. Since then we have realized that all things are in God's hands.

This study was started before the world changed for us and is now to be given to you.

Sincerely,
Donald Earl Frith

SECTION 1

This is a great mystery.

The mystery machine

We are taking our study from the verse that we find in Ephesians 5:32; "**This is a great mystery: that I speak concerning Christ and the church.**" Since God called this a great mystery in Ephesians chapter 5 we will go ahead and use that same term. We will take a tour of the mystery in our study.

We are going to create a conceptual mystery machine. We will break this down into the following parts; we will be looking at what we will call tire one, followed by tire two, and the axle that ties these two tires together. We will then look at the front wheels and axle. We will apply some axle grease. We will connect a steering wheel. Then we will take a world tour using our mystery machine.

Let us take a moment and say a prayer turning this whole project over into God's hands. "Our Father we pray that You will help us as we study and look at what is meant by this great mystery. We now turn all our thoughts, all our words over to You. Stop us from including that which is not from You, and help us to include those things which You have for somebody who is reading this book. Thank You for giving us your Holy Spirit that He may lead us in understanding of what You have put in Your Word. We turn these over to You in the name of Jesus our Savior and Lord. Amen."

We will not be talking about doctrines, dogmas, or denominational beliefs. We want to be like the men of Berea found in Act 17:11; "**.... They received the word with all readiness of mind, and searched the Scriptures daily, whether those things were so.**" Let us study and hear with open minds and open hearts.

We have a natural sin tendency to see our version of the Bible as more accurate than someone else's version and therefore they should listen to us. This version context debate tends to lead us away from hearing and believing, and into pride of who has the most accurate and better biblical content.

Another contextual debate which leads us into pride is the study and knowledge of the Hebrew and Greek languages. Our prideful tendency is to think that since we know the Hebrew or the Greek, we know more than others. We will not get into the meaning of the Greek or Hebrew words.

We will make an observation about those languages and why God used them for the Bible as it pertains to our study. In both languages the nouns used have both a masculine and feminine construction and content.

'The easiest way to keep from truth is to assume that we already know the truth.' We will be looking at what may seem to be common ground from the teachings of others. So with an open mind we will study some of the intent of some well-worn Bible verses.

Back tire one (the wife)

(NKJV – New King James Version)
Scripture references
Colossians 3:18 Ephesians 5:22-24 First Peter 3:1-6

We have pointed out that the title of our study comes from Ephesians 5:32; "**this is a great mystery: that I speak concerning Christ and the church.**" We are going to take a journey into a mystery called 'Christ and the church' in the form of a mystery machine.

In both Colossians 3:18 and Ephesians 5:22 we have as one of the back power wheels; "**wives, submit yourselves unto your own husbands,**" If you are under an understanding that we would be studying the differences between male and female, you have come to the right study. Let us create our machine from the Scriptures.

Let us check and see if our tire is properly inflated. Colossians 3:18 completes the statement with; '**as it is fit in the Lord.**" (3:18B) This tire is said to be properly fitted in the design of the Lord. So one of the things that we will be examining is how this is fitted in the Lord.

Ephesians 5:22 completes the statement with; "**as unto the Lord.**" Then continuing the thought in 5:23, we are told why this submission is as unto the Lord. "**For the husband is the head of the wife, even as Christ is the head of the church: and He is the Savior of the body.**"

As we presented earlier the Greek language has masculine and feminine noun texts. The word 'head' turns out to be a feminine noun. So as we identify the difference between masculine and feminine, this concept of the head will come more into focus.

Ephesians 5:24 finishes up the concept with; "**therefore as the church is subject unto Christ, so the wives to their own husbands in everything.**" We will find a more complete understanding of this concept as we get into the masculine and feminine discussion.

First Peter 3:1-2 we read; "Wives, **likewise, be in subjection to your own husbands; that, if any obey not the word, they also may without the word be won by the conversation of**

3

the wise; while they behold your chaste conversation with fear." In first Peter 3 we see how this tire functions in our spiritual mystery machine.

First Peter 3:5 also tells us about wives of the Old Testament; "**for after this manner in the old time the holy women also, who trusted in God, adorned themselves, being in subjection unto their own husbands:**". In 3:6 we are even given an example of such a wife who led her husband to God. "**Even as Sarah obeyed Abraham, calling him Lord:**" (3:6A) It is then that by the subjection of a wife to a husband as unto the Lord, a husband who does not follow or know God can be brought to God, by how the wife understands and operates within this concept.

We are called the 'children of Abraham' if we have faith in God. Moreover in 3:6 subjective wives are also called; "**whose daughter's ye are, as long as you do well, and are not afraid with any amazement.**" (3:6B) We are told that God chose Abram, but that is after Abram chose God. We are now told that it was Sarah who brought Abram to God.

Tire one is the wife, who is submissive to her own husband in everything as being submissive unto the Lord and being properly fitted in the Lord. Such a wife can bring a conversion to her husband by her actions.

Back tire two (the husband)

Scripture references
Colossians 3:19 Ephesians 5:25–30 First
Peter 3:7 First Corinthians 7:3–4

In Colossians 3:19 and Ephesians 5:25 let us now check out the other back tire. "**Husbands, love your wives,**". Back in Colossians 3:19 the statement is finished with; "**and be not bitter against them.**" (3:19B) Can a husband love his wife and still be bitter against her for something he thinks she may have said or done? Bitterness is not the opposite of love; however, the wife may pick up on the husband's bitterness and not on his love. So husbands are told not to be bitter when they love their wives.

In Ephesians 5:25 the statement is finished with; "**even as Christ also loved the church, and gave Himself for it;**" (5:25B) We are given in 5:26-27 a reason why Christ died for the church. Not because of any value that the church has innately. "**That He might sanctify and cleanse it with the washing of water by the word, that He might present to Himself a glorious church, not having spot, or wrinkle, or any such thing; but that it should be holy and without blemish.**" He died that He may cleanse, sanctify, and present to Himself a glorious and holy church.

We notice that the original statement was written to the husband. So let us read the statement for the husband; that the husband may sanctify and cleanse his wife with the washing of water by the word, that the husband might present his wife to himself a glorious body, not having spot, or wrinkle, or any such physical things; but that his wife should be holy and without internal blemish.

To further emphasize this thought Ephesians 5:28-30 continues with; "**so ought men to love their wives as their own bodies. He that loves his wife loves himself. For no man ever yet hated his own flesh; but nourisheth it and cherisheth it, even as the Lord the church: for we are members of his body, of his flesh, and of his bones.**" In rephrasing this last statement for the husband we read; for the wife is a member of the husband's body, his flesh, and his bones.

First Peter 3:7 we read; "**likewise, ye husbands, dwell with [her] according to knowledge, giving honor unto the wife, as unto the weaker vessel, and as being heirs together of the grace of life;**". (3:7A) What is the purpose of the husband's love for his wife? The husband is to dwell with the wife according to knowledge. If a husband was in agreement with the world's concept, '**Women, you can't live with them and you can't live without them.**' Or any other such thought, he needs to get on his knees and to ask God for forgiveness and for knowledge. Why?

In 3:7 we are told; "**that your prayers be not hindered.**" (3:7B) Could it be possible that our prayers are not as effective as they should be because husbands do not dwell with their wives according to knowledge?

Let us now see if the tires are equally inflated. First Corinthians 7:3 we read; "**that the husband render unto the wife due benevolence: and likewise also the wife unto the husband.**" We see that not only are we to give benevolence to each other, but we are to give it when it is due. This word benevolence is another feminine noun.

Axle (joining of the wife and husband)

Scripture references
Ephesians 5:31- 33

Let us now place the back tires on an axle to place on the mystery machine. Ephesians 5:31 states; **"for this cause shall a man leave his father and mother, and shall be joined unto his wife, and they two shall be one flesh."** (5:31) For what cause? For the cause of joining by subjection in love to function in balance as one unit.

At this point 5:32 we are given the mystery for which we are creating our mystery machine; **"this is a great mystery: but I speak concerning Christ and the church."** And to observe that our tires and axle function together properly 5:33; **"nevertheless let every one of you in particular so love his wife even as himself; and the wife that she reverence her husband."** (5:33) We observe that the husband is to love his wife and the wife is to reverence her husband.

Front tires and axle (joining of the male and female)

Scripture references
Matthew 19:3-8 Mark 10:2-9

Let us check out the front tires and axle to our mystery machine. In Matthew 19:3 we find that; **"the Pharisees also came under Him, tempting Him, and saying to Him, is it lawful for a man to put away his wife for every cause?"** We then read 19:4; **"and He answered and said unto them, have you not read, that He which made at the beginning made them male and female,"** [(19:4A)] So we have our front tires.

Now for the axle, Matthew 19:4-5; **"And said, for this cause shall a man leave father and mother, and should be joined to his wife: and they twain shall be one flesh?** [(19:4B)] **Wherefore they are no more twain, but one flesh. What therefore God hath joined together, let no man put asunder."** For what reasons were they brought together? They were brought together for the reason that they were made male and female.

Looking at Mark 10:3-5 we are told; **"..... and He answered and said unto them, what did Moses command you? And they said, Moses suffered to write a bill of divorcement, and to put away. And Jesus answered and said unto them, for the hardness of your heart he wrote you this precept."** Let us finish looking at our tires and axles one more time with Mark 10:6-9. **"But from the beginning of the creation God made them male and female. For this cause shall a man leave his father and mother, and cleave to his wife; and they twain shall be one flesh: so then they are no more twain, but one flesh. What therefore God had joined together, let no man put asunder."**

We notice that we use the same tires and axles for front and back. The only difference being that the placement of the back tires were classified as husband and wife, and the power implied thereof. While the placement of the same tires as the front tires were classified as male and female with the guiding principle that applies.

This union of tires and axles, functions as the driving force in husband and wife, and becomes a directional force as male and female.

As we go on our mystery tour we will want to keep these two unique functions in mind.

Grease

Scripture references
Mark 10:10-12 Matthew 5:31-32 Matthew 19:8-9 Luke 16:18

To help our axles run smoothly we are going to need to add grease. Since grease is messy, dirty, or for no better way of saying it downright greasy, we will examine the grease first, and then apply it to the axles.

In Mark 10:10-12 we are told; "**and in the house His disciples asked Him again of the same." And He saith unto them, "whosoever shall put away his wife, and marry another, commits adultery against her. And if a woman shall put away her husband, and be married to another, she commits adultery.**" They wanted to make sure they understood, so they asked him again about reasons for divorcement.

In Matthew 5:31-32 we are told; "**it has been said, whosoever shall put away his wife, let him give her a writing of divorcement: but I say unto you, that whosoever shall put away his wife, saving for the cause of fornication, causeth her to commit adultery: and whosoever shall marry her that is divorced commits adultery.**" As we are adding the grease to the axles, we find that the husband who divorces his wife commits adultery, and causes his wife to commit adultery also; as was shown in Matthew 5.

Also the wife who divorces her husband commits adultery, as is shown in Mark 10.

In Matthew 19:8-9 we are told; "...... He **saith unto them, Moses because of the hardness of your hearts suffered you to put away your wives: that from the beginning it was not so. And I say unto you, whosoever shall put away his wife, except for fornication, and shall marry another, commits adultery: and whosoever marries her which is put away doth commit adultery.**" She who marries a divorced husband, or he who marries a divorced wife commits adultery, as in Matthew 19 and Luke 16.

In Luke 16:18 we are told; "**whosoever put away his wife, and marries another, commits adultery: and whosoever marries**

her that is put away from [her] husband commits adultery."
We notice that not only does the one who causes the divorce commits
adultery, and the one who is divorced commits adultery, but anyone
who joins with either of these two also commits adultery.

What is the difference between adultery and fornication? In
our study we find that adultery is the separation of the tire from the
axle, while fornication is the placement of the tire on another axle.
Whether the adultery or fornication is done with the agreement of
both parties, we find that this is not in the agreement of God's design
as explained in Christ and the church.

Steering wheel

Scripture references
Matthew 19:10-12

In turning back to Matthew 19:10 we observe that the disciples made a conclusion which the world tends to agree with; "..... **His disciples say unto Him, if the case of the man be so with [his] wife, it is not good to marry.**" We will now attach a steering wheel to our axles.

This is what the world says; 'why get married, let us just live together and see if it works out.'

We are given almost a mystery answer. Since we are in our mystery machine let us hear what is said in 19:11. "**But He said unto them, all cannot receive this saying, save to whom it is given.**" So we ask ourselves to what saying is he referring?

He continues on in 19:12 by giving us this statement; "**for there are some eunuchs, which were so born from mother's womb: and there are some eunuchs, which are made eunuchs of men: and there be some eunuchs, which have made themselves eunuchs for the kingdom of heaven sake. He that is able to receive, let him receive.**" Describing eunuchs as someone who is singularly set apart for a purpose, we understand that there are some who are to be single from their mother's womb. A look at John the Baptist is this type of singleness. He was called a voice calling out in the wilderness.

There are some who are single because of men. A look at Samuel and his mother confirms this type of singleness. He was given to God by his mother.

And some make themselves single for the work of the kingdom of God. A look at Paul confirms this type of singleness. He gave himself over to God.

For him who is able to receive the call of being single let him receive the singleness, all others marry. Singleness is, as far as God directs, only for those who are set apart for a purpose. For everyone else the man is to leave father and mother, and join unto his wife, and they became one in the grace of life.

Motor

Scripture references
Genesis 2:24 Genesis 4:1-2,25

Then we read in Genesis 2:24; **"therefore shall a man leave his father and his mother, and shall cleave unto his wife: and they shall be one flesh."** Let us add the motor to our mystery machine and start our journey. The first time we read about this mystery is in Genesis where God brings the female to the male and he calls her woman.

We notice that this statement was not made by Adam, but by Him who made them male and female from the beginning.[see Matthew 19] Had Adam made this statement or repeated God's statement? There appears to be a question of what did Adam know, what was he talking about? After all, who were Adams father and mother? And why was it not stated that the female should leave her father and mother and join unto her husband.

If we start to accept what most of the church body accepts, that man is generic for human, then the wife becomes generic for spouse. This allows the world and the church to accept that a male husband can join to his male wife, and a female husband can join to her female wife. The sin of the church is not the sin of the male to male or female to female. But it is the acceptance of this redefinition that God made them male and female, and the male shall join to the female, and they shall be one flesh.

Let us start our motor. In Genesis 4:1 we read; **"Now Adam knew Eve his wife; and she conceived, and [she] bare Cain, and [she] said, I have gotten a man from the Lord."** Wait a minute. Adam knew Eve. She conceived, bore Cain, and said that the Lord gave her a man.

Continuing in Genesis 4:2; **"and she again bare his brother Abel."** Were Cain and Abel twins? When we separate what Eve said about Cain for a second we read; **"and Adam knew Eve his wife; and she conceived, and bare Cain, ... and she again bare his brother Abel."** They were both born from the same conception. However, in Genesis 4:25 we read; **"and Adam knew his wife again; and she bare a son, and called his name Seth: for God,**

hath appointed me another seed instead of Able, who Cain slew." You may think that is obvious that Adam knew Eve again, but the Holy Spirit wants us to be aware of the two conceptions.

The function of this motor is so important to God that he included it in the Ten **Commandments** in Exodus 20:12. "**honor thy father and thy mother: that thy days may be long upon the land which the Lord thy God giveth thee.**" We could go into any bookstore, library, medical catalog, medical website, or other sources and pick out information on what is called by the world reproduction. But he gave us some hints that there is more to reproduction than a man knowing a woman in her conceiving and bearing a child.

Let us look at "**God, hath appointed me another seed**".

SECTION 2

Here is our world tour in the mystery machine:

Stop one (God's choice):

We will be making several stops on our mystery tour, but not all the stops we could make on this trip. The foundation for our first stop through the concepts of the world comes from everydayhealth.com.

From that website we find information on ovaries. At birth a woman's ovaries already contain several hundred thousand undeveloped eggs. The eggs are not called into action until puberty. Roughly once a month ovulation occurs; starting at puberty and lasting until menopause the ovaries release an egg into her fallopian tubes.

We are told that from birth a female has all the eggs that she will ever have in her life. This means that the ovary of the baby girl contains all of her eggs. At puberty she starts to ovulate one egg every month. Some studies are being made at clinics where scientists are looking for answers to the questions; which egg is provided, in which order, and what decides that egg that month. Eve tells us that she had received a male child from the Lord. The Lord decides which egg.

From the website we find the following information on testicles. A man's testicles at puberty produces male sex cells called sperm. Starting at puberty, testicles produce testosterone, the male sex hormone. Once started a man's sperm production continues throughout his life. Sexually mature males produce millions of sperm cells each day.

Since it only takes one sperm at conception, why so many? In clinics scientists are trying to answer that question, as well as answer the question of what determines which sperm cell joins with the egg. Is it just first come first serve? Is it the law of the fittest, or the strongest, or the biggest? Eve tells us that she had received a male child from the Lord. The Lord decides which sperm.

For our first stop in our tour we found that the Lord decides which egg from the female and which sperm cell from the male He uses to make you. Your mother and father were chosen by God for your creation, and in honoring them you honor God.

Stop two (God's structures)

The second stop on our journey is looking at information from Bionet news where we will point out some of the scientific findings of the physical differences between male and female. The first one we are going to deal with is the brain.

The male brain gives man the edge in dealing with physical things and theorems. The female brain is organized to respond more sensitively to all sensory stimuli. Women do better than men on tests of verbal ability.

Wow, the male brain is designed to deal with things, and the female brain is '**organized**' to deal with stimuli. Picking up on that subject of stimuli; females are physically equipped to receive a wider range of sensory information, to connect and relate that information with greater ability, to place dominance on personal relationships, and to communicate. While cultural influences may reinforce these strengths, the advantages are innate.

Females are '**organized**' to take that stimuli and primarily apply it to relationships and communications. We also find that the differences are noticeable in the very first hours after birth. It has been shown that girl babies are much more interested in people and faces. Boys seem just as happy with an object dangled in front of them. Girls say their first words and learn to speak in short sentences earlier than boys. They are generally more articulate in their pre-school years. They read earlier and do better in coping with the building blocks of language like grammar, punctuation, and spelling.

Now to help females in this 'organizing' of stimuli we find that even from birth there is a difference in hearing. We find women hear words better than men. When the sexes are compared, women show a greater sensitivity to sound. A dripping tap will get the woman out of bed even before it wakes up the man. Six times as many girls as boys can sing in tune. They are also more adept in noticing small changes in volume, which goes a long way to explaining a woman's superior sensitivity to that 'tone of voice' which their male partners are so often accused of using.

Also to help females in this '**organizing**' of stimuli we find that even from birth there is a difference in vision. Men and women even see things differently. Women can see better in the dark. They are more sensitive to the red end of the color spectrum. They see more red hues than men. They have a better visual memory. Men see clearer than women in bright light.

Regarding the difference in vision intriguing results also showed that men tend to be literally 'blinkered'. They see in a narrow field – a mild tunnel vision - with greater concentration on depth discernment. They have a better sense of perception than women. However, women quite literally take in the bigger picture. They have wider peripheral vision. They have more of the receptor rods and cones in the retina at the back of the eyeball, to receive a wider arc of visual input.

Wow, men see specific goals. Women see everything and their eyes are even designed to see everything. Women respond quicker and more intensely to pain, although their overall resistance to long-term discomfort is greater than men. In a sample of young adults, women displayed 'overwhelmingly' greater sensitivity to pressure on the skin over every part of the body. From childhood women have a demonstrative sensitivity so much greater than men that in these tests there are no overlaps between the scores of the two sexes. The least sensitive woman is more responsive than the most sensitive man.

We find out that even the most aware man is not as responsive as is the least perceptive female. Yet the world wants the two to be the same. God has made them different for a purpose. And God has made you male or female with special physical gifts for a purpose.

Stop three (God's gift – the brain)

The third stop on our journey is to study the cells of the one organ in the human body which cannot be replaced, cannot be repaired, and cannot be restarted. This organ is the human brain. Since 1965 death has been defined by brain death (lack of brain function). Until 1965 death was whenever the body ceased to function. This was determined by what was called '**staying up with the dead**', where the body was watched for one of two things to happen. Either the person would arise in a living state or the body would start to stink.

With the ceased function of the brain as our medical definition of clinical death we will visit the **<u>Prenatal Diagnosis</u>** study in which they started with a question. Are there actually significant differences between a girl's brain and a boy's brain?

Beginning in the womb sex differences in the brain was apparent. A developing baby boy's testicles start churning out testosterone in substantial quantities midway through the pregnancy. This serum testosterone concentration is equivalent to those seen in young adult men. By enzymes within the brain, the sex hormones bind to brain tissue and begin to transform it. Between 18 and 26 weeks gestation, the developing brain is permanently and irreversibly altered.

The difference between a female brain and a male brain can be distinguished in a regular ultrasound examination when a woman is 26 weeks pregnant. Once changed the difference is permanent. Examinations made at birth shows that a child is born with a male brain or a female brain. Postnatal experiences will not change your brain from male to female, or vice a versa. An experience even as extreme as a physical castration, does not change the brain.

We are to understand that there is no female brain or male brain transformed to the other sex no matter what is done physically to the body. This means that no female born with a female brain was inadvertently born a male. Also no male born with a male brain was inadvertently born a female. At 26 weeks in the womb God has set the male and the female based on the formation of the brain. Any other choice to be male or female, contrary to God's creation of the brain, is only that just a choice and not a fact.

Donald Frith

From the **Journal of Neuropathology and Experimental Neurology** we look at the structural sex differences in the human brain.

We understand that a research team recently compared brain tissue from the brains of young girls and young boys. They found that sex differences in the structure of the brain were obvious, even in babies--especially in babies. The differences in the photomicrographs of the brain tissue are so dramatic that they are readily visible to the naked eye. So we see that the brain of the male and the female not only function differently but are visibly structured differently. God created the brain to be different in structure, function, and goal between male and female.

Stop four (God's building materials)

Information from an article at News–Medical.net indicates that the brain's white matter may determine susceptibility to chronic pain. According to the researchers who used brain scans the structure of the brain may predict whether a person will suffer chronic low back pain. Results support the growing idea that the brain plays a crucial role in chronic pain. This may lead to changes in the way doctors treat chronic pain patients.

The Apkarian laboratory study showed that in persistent pain subjects the volume of gray matter in the brain decreased over the same year. The central bodies and branched antenna, or dendrites, of nerve cells reside in the gray matter area of the brain. This study showed that brain activity could be used to predict whether a subject recovered or experienced persistent pain.

The researchers used a scanning technique called the fusion tensor imaging (DTI). DTI measures the structure of white matter, the nerve cell wires, or axons, which connect brain cells in different parts of the brain.

To further understand what we are talking about we need to look at what is the definition of white brain matter. From the MEDLINEplus website we find the definition of white matter is tissue found in the brain containing nerve fibers (axons). Many axons are surrounded by a type of fat called myelin which gives the white matter its color. Myelin acting as an insulator plays an important role in the speed of nerve signaling.

We find from the Wikipedia.org website the definition for gray matter as a major component of the central nervous system. It consists of neuronal cell bodies, neuropil (dendrites and unmyelinated axons), glial cells (astroglia and oligodendrcytes), and capillaries. Gray matter contains neural cell bodies but does not contain the myelinated axon tracks. The whiteness of myelin creates the brain cell color differences. In living tissue the color comes from capillary blood vessels and neuronal cell bodies. Gray matter actually has a gray-brown color.

Why the interest in gray verses white matter of the brain? From an article in the science daily.com website titled 'Intelligence in men and women is a gray and white matter'. We find that first there is no apparent discrepancy in the general intelligence between the sexes. A UC [University of California] Irvine study found significant differences in the brain <u>areas</u> where males and females manifest their intelligence. The study showed that women have more white matter related to intellect. Men have more gray matter related to intellect. This revealed that the atomic structure of no single neuron determines general intelligence. Different types of brain cell designs are capable of producing comparable intellectual performance.

What we are told basically is that the man's mind has more gray matter which is related to goal driven thinking. The woman's mind has more white matter. This is related with relational thinking. Men have approximately 6.5 times the amount of gray matter related to general intelligence than women. Women have nearly 10 times the amount of white matter related to intelligence than men. Gray matter represents the information processing centers in the brain. The white matter represents the networking of - or connections between - those processing centers.

This may explain why men tend to excel in tasks requiring more local processing (like mathematics). Women tend to excel at absorbing and combining information from the scattered gray-matter regions of the brain, such as required for language skill. Moreover these two very different neurological pathways and activity centers result in parallel overall performance. On broad measures of cognitive ability, such as those found on intelligence tests, they display comparatively equal intelligence.

The study acknowledged regional differences with intelligence. For example, in women 84 percent of their gray-matter regions and 86 percent of their white-matter regions, which were involved with intellectual performance, were found in the brain's frontal lobes. Respectively men compared to 45 percent and zero percent. The gray matter driving male intellectual performance is distributed throughout more of the brain.

The male and female brains are structured differently, are linked to different hormones, are made of different amounts of the different types of brain matter, which God has incorporated into the male and female brains. God has made it so that even with a different structure, a different goal, a different hormone, and different brain matter, God has given the capability of men and women to have equal but dissimilar intelligence.

Stop five (God's brain structures (different but same))

We have learned that the brain is structured differently for male and female. This structure difference is from the very first stem cell at conception. Next stop on our journey is to look at the structure of the brain, both the type of cells and the functions of the cells. We found that by 28 weeks in the womb the brain has been altered into the cells making the male brain entirely different than the female brain. We also found that this was done by the flow of estrogen and testosterone in the brain.

One of the effects on the brain is the changing physically of the type of cells which make up the brain. Over the years during autopsies of the brain, the cells showed a gray color and the brain cells were referred to as gray brain cells. During the more current advanced studies on the brain a different brain cell appeared. It was colored white and labeled as the white brain cells. White cells in the brain are shown to work in the organizing of emotions, stimuli, perceptions, connections to the body's functions: such as speech, action, emotions, etc. From the creation of the first brain cell were white brain cells. The gray cells in the brain are shown to work to limit and narrow the function of the brain in relation to stimulus outside the body.

In research and study it has turned out that more than half of the structure of the female brain is made of white brain cells. Whereas, the male brain contains less than 1% white brain cells. The brains of the male and the female are physically wired differently using different myelinated axons and unmyelinated material. Further studies have shown that the function throughout the brain varies between male and female.

Let us study how this happens. Let us review what we saw at 28 weeks. As the hormones are generated and sent through the brain of the unborn child the male child's brain is physically altered. Up until that point in time all brain cells are white brain cells. When the testosterone hits the male brain at least two observable things happen.

The first observable effect upon the male brain is that most of the white brain cells are destroyed. The testosterone keeps the brain from forming anymore white brain cells. Since they are gone from the brain before birth the action of testosterone at puberty does not alter the structural makeup of the male brain.

The second observable effect upon the male brain is that most of the neural pathways between the two hemispheres of the brain are destroyed. So the brain is literally cut in two. This action occurs again in the male at puberty causing the brain again to be physically cut in two. A male needs to be trained to handle this major process in his body.

Much more is being found about the brain, however to move on we will make one last observation. The male and the female do not think from the same parts of the brain or in the same fashion. To assume that a male can understand what or how a female is thinking degrades them both. Likewise, to assume that a female can understand what or how a male is thinking confuses them both.

Stop six (God's first building block – the Zygote)

The next stop on our tour is called the '**zygote**'. When God's chosen egg and sperm unites, it creates an embryonic cell called a stem cell (zygote). Since 2000 scientists have made intensive studies looking to explain where, how, and why these stem cells work.

Let us take a little trip back in time and observe a scientist studying zygotes of every creature he can get his hands upon. He observed that their '**functions**' are all the same. They all '**looked**' the same. He concluded that there must be an '**original embryonic stem cell**' for all living creatures that somehow they evolved into the individual species we have now. This also means that once this cellular determination key is found, it then can be adjusted to improve or evolve humanity. This theory is called evolution. This evolutionary theory has been called '**from the goo to you by way of the zoo**'. The Bible states that man looks on the outward appearance, while God looks on the inward appearance.

Proving this evolutionary theory requires monthly tests made, sanctioned, required, and reviewed by the government. In doing these tests the government and scientists actually prove that evolution does not exist, and cannot exist. These tests fail in every attempt to prove evolution exists. The food industry performs these tests required by the government. You and I would not have any kind of packaged pre-prepared storable food if the 'evolutionary theory' was true.

What is a stem cell, where does it exist, and what does it do? The very first cell in any human being has been defined as the stem cell. From the Wikipedia web site we find that stem cells are <u>undifferentiated</u> <u>biological cells</u> that can <u>differentiate</u> into specialized cells and can <u>divide</u> (through <u>mitosis</u>) to produce more stem cells. They are found in multi-cellular <u>organisms</u>. In <u>mammals</u>, there are two broad types of stem cells. <u>Embryonic stem cells</u>, are isolated in the <u>inner cell mass</u> of <u>blastocysts</u>. <u>Adult stem cells</u> are found in various tissues. In <u>adult</u> organisms, stem cells and <u>progenitor cells</u> act as a repair system for the body. They replenish adult tissues. In a developing embryo, stem cells can separate into all the specialized cells—ectoderm, endoderm and mesoderm. They also maintain the normal turnover of regenerative organs, such as blood, skin, or intestinal tissues.

There are three accessible sources of <u>autologous</u> adult stem cells in humans.

1. Bone marrow, which requires extraction by *harvesting*, that is, drilling into bone (typically the <u>femur</u> [thighs] or <u>iliac crest</u> [hip]).
2. Adipose tissue (lipid cells [fat]), which requires extraction by liposuction.
3. Blood, which requires extraction through <u>apheresis</u>, wherein blood is drawn from the donor (similar to a blood donation), passed through a machine that extracts the stem cells, and returns other portions of the blood to the donor.

Stem cells can also be taken from the <u>umbilical cord blood</u> just after birth. Of all stem cell types, autologous harvesting involves the least risk. By definition, autologous cells are obtained from one's own body. Just as one may bank his or her own blood for elective surgical procedures.

Adult stem cells are routinely used in medical therapies. One example is <u>bone marrow transplantation</u>. Stem cells can be <u>artificially grown</u> and transformed (differentiated) into specialized cell types with characteristics consistent with cells of various tissues such as muscles or nerves. Embryonic <u>cell lines</u> and <u>autologous</u> embryonic stem cells generated through <u>therapeutic cloning</u> have also been proposed as promising candidates for future therapies; especially hopeful to repair spinal injuries.

Wow! God made a cell which He can change into any one of your needed diversified cells! God has also hidden these special stem cells in places where He can get to them quicker and easier. [Yet they are still protected from outside influences.]

We have seen through our stops God has made us using our parents, and designed us specifically to function in a certain manner. Not only are our cells unique, our bodies unique, our brains unique, but we also find on our next stop that God has made even the code in the very cells unique!

Stop seven (God's unique code – DNA)

We now move into the inner construction of these stem cells in what is now called DNA (Deoxyriboneucleic Acid). When DNA was introduced and studied they used the evolutionary theory to say that the DNA of humans and primates are so close that there had to be an earlier DNA form connecting the two types of DNA.

DNA was found to have excess structure which was called trash DNA and theorized that this was DNA left over from man evolving from primates. In March 2010 scientist proved that some of the so-called trash DNA is, from the very first embryonic stem cell, actually the identification of the gender and the species of that cell (article in ScienceDaily.com).

In other words from the first stem cell a human is a human, and will not, and cannot be anything other than human, no matter what is done to that cell. Also from the first stem cell a man is a man, and a woman is a woman, no matter what is done to that cell. While man looks on the outside God looks on the inside. God made you a man or woman from the very first stem cell of your existence.

Even in the construction by DNA of male and female, God made a difference in what is used to construct a male versus what is used to construct a female. This difference was found and titled the X chromosome and the Y chromosome.

A show presented on the Science Channel titled **'children without sex'** went into the possibility of how now a child can be made outside the womb using DNA. The premise was that this could lead to the possibility of having children without the pain and suffering of having the child in the womb, by having a child in an artificial scientific created womb. The discussion went on to present how science can now take the DNA from two women and make a baby.

But they did admit that there was one problem that they have not been able to solve. The problem is the Y chromosome. They cannot take sperm from two men and produce a baby. They have to have an egg. Why is this? What is so special about the Y chromosome? What part does it play in the construction of a man or a woman? Scientists admitted that they could not make a Y chromosome from an X chromosome.

Looking at a website called brainrules.com, we are given the sizes and the information stored in the X chromosome and the Y chromosome. The X chromosome codes nearly 45 times more proteins than the Y chromosome -- most of them involved in brain development. It has 1200 to 1500 genes, while the Y is down to 100 genes.

We are told that a good part of the difference between the X chromosome and the Y chromosome deals with the development of the brain which we went into in some detail. So we see that the Y chromosome does not have the same genes that are in the X chromosome. The Y chromosome does not perform the same function as the X chromosome. Two functions of the Y chromosome are determining the sex and blood type of the baby.

When God constructs a female in the womb he literally has 1200 genes too many. What does He do with these extra genes? With two X chromosomes, only half of the genes are needed. The female brain deactivates them, randomly choosing between genes from mom and genes from dad.

The next comment we are going to disagree with slightly. This cell solves this problem by activating one of them in a process called 'X-inactivation'. It is random. Either one of these can be silenced.

We disagree with the concept that this is random. God has the choice of using the best of both sets of X chromosomes from the mother and from the father, to improve and enhance the capability of the woman to be better able to function in all the physical requirements that she needs in '**organizing**' all the stimuli around her.

The male who has received the X chromosome from his mother and the Y chromosome from his father does not have this 'X-inactivation'. Because of this the male brain always comes from the X chromosomes of the mother. So a male is literally **"a mama's boy"** in the structure and function of the brain. Women's brains formed from genes from either X chromosome are said to be "**by gendered**".

This means that some of the brain's disorders are being determined to be gender related. Some brain disorders divide along gender lines. For example women have far higher incidences of post-traumatic stress disorder and anorexia than men. Men are more often affected by addiction and attention-deficit disorder.

God even made certain parts of the brain anatomically different. Areas of the brain are bigger or smaller depending on gender. It is not fully known whether this difference transfers to behavior. For example, it is common to say women are more emotional than men. Men have a larger amygdala, which is heavily involved in motion.

Some of the neuroanatomical variations between a man and woman brains are:

1. The frontal cortex is bigger, and more complex in women.
2. The parietal cortex is bigger, and more complex in men.
3. The corpus collosum show observable structural differences.
4. The hippocampus is larger, and faster in women.
5. The amygdale is larger in men.
6. Serotonin production is larger, and faster in men.

As we see God has made a difference between male and female in structure, in function, in purpose, and in His need, and for His use. Our next two stops are to look at the concept of masculine, and then to look at the concept of feminine.

Stop eight (God made masculine)

The world of science is finding that there are major differences between the masculine and feminine. Let us look into the concept of masculine. At this point we can agree with what we are told in the Bible that God made man in his own image, and in His own likeness made He them, male and female made He them. Looking at some of the information today about the differences between male and female, we get an impression that the male and the female are to function differently. The male is conceptually driven and narrow minded.

How do these differences function as far as relationships between male and female? To get an answer to this question we are going to change topics from the structural differences to the conceptual differences. This means we are going to change from looking at the male and the female to looking at the masculine and the feminine.

In doing this we need to come up with a definition of what is masculine and what is feminine. Keep in mind when we do these definitions we have to look at the physical 'kind' to get a clue as to the conceptual.

We find out from the scientific community that the masculine male thinks in a "blinkered viewed" form. We found out that he is goal orientated and tends to eliminate, ignore, or not perceive all the stimuli that are around him. We also found that his brain was literally cut in two and restructured, and is formed strictly from his mother's DNA.

Having stopped at the various locations, we could say that the masculine lacks a good part of what the feminine possesses. Moreover, we also realize that according to Genesis God put Adam to sleep and made from Adam's rib Eve. So whatever Adam lacks Eve possesses, but that also means that whatever Eve lacks Adam possesses.

So what we're going to do is identify the masculine as being the structure, the goal, the purpose, the drive, the design, and the outward appearance that God sees of 'man'. We also can see why man was told to leave mother and father. God made the masculine limited in his construction yet highly focused as to purpose. We can see why God placed him as head of the wife.

Stop nine (God made feminine)

Let us look into the concept of feminine. The feminine mind is absorbing and organizing of stimuli. We realized that not only was Eve made from Adam's rib, but she was made for a purpose of receiving and organizing the entire world around her. Her structure, her brain, and even her sensitivity were designed to handle this function.

This means that when the Bible says in Genesis that God brought Eve to Adam there is more involved than just His bringing the female to the male. What God has done is brought that part of Adam which he could use to respond to the stimuli around him, to him in a separate physical package.

In the view of God her relationship to Adam was stated very plainly she was to be the helpmate for Adam. In other words she was to organize the entire world around them for Adam, so Adam was able to make decisions as to the goals they would make for their lives.

This also explains why Satan went to Eve rather than Adam, and why Eve was said to be tempted while Adam fell into sin.

We have one more stop before we are done with our tour, that is the masculine needs and the feminine needs.

Stop 10 (God appointed masculine/feminine needs)

To understand this a little bit better we need to picture what masculine and feminine needs look like, how they function, and what their needs are.

To do this we are going to turn to the feminine and masculine nouns. We found as we were looking at some of the early verses there was a use of feminine nouns which we did not understand nor did we comprehend what they implied.

We're going to turn to nouns in our normal everyday vocabulary to display this concept of masculine and feminine nouns, and how God deals with this concept.

Let us look at the words in our English language which defines that dwelling where you live. If you were telling somebody how to get to where you live, you would describe to them what we call your house. The concept of house being where you live as is seen by others.

In the Hebrew or the Greek this noun would be considered a masculine noun displaying the existence of what an item is. This is a house, this is where you reside, and this is what associates you with other people.

If we were to define this structure by its function we would call this our home. The very idea of a home is what functions inside of the structure of the house. It is used for the inside the structure, does not lead to the structure, does not explain the structure, nor does it describe the structure.

This word home would be considered a feminine noun. Thus the feminine noun is being the internal functional use of the external masculine noun. So we would look at the masculine noun house and the feminine noun home as being the exact same thing but for two different entirely different purposes.

We notice that the masculine noun is the outward goal orientated single-minded directed concept, while the feminine noun is the internal organized totally perceived complete concept. It turns out this is also the functions of masculine and feminine.

Starting with the concept of need when we deal with this masculine and feminine, it has been determined that there are what is called rhythms in life. Some of these rhythms we know as daily rhythms, such as a 24-hour rhythm, such as a 60 minute rhythm, such as a 60 second rhythm, such as a seven-day week, and other rhythms that have been defined.

We are going to look at three rhythms that have been identified which do in fact function in male or female, masculine or feminine, or man and woman. These are actual rhythms which have an impact on our physical lives; they are the physical, the mental, and the emotional.

We found that the female (feminine) is more sensitive than the male (masculine). The needs of these daily rhythms are the same for both. Yet the requirements to fill these needs are going to be greatly different.

It turns out that the female because of the way she is structured both mentally and physically, must at all times do what we call think (mental), feel (emotional), and act (physical). She cannot do just one of those at any point in time, but that she must do all three of those at the same time. It has been shown that she cannot spend any second in her life without doing all three.

The male (masculine) because of the structural changes in his brain at birth, the structural differences in his body, and the use of his brain causes him to be able to do only one of these three things at a time. He cannot do two or three at the same time. God has made it so that most of the time he is not even doing one of those three things.

This causes confusion between men and women. Women will never understand or comprehend how the man can exist without doing one of those three things. Likewise a man will never understand how the woman has to do all three of those things at the same time all the time.

It has been said that due to the structure of the female always connecting stimuli data into an organized pattern so that she has more than four times as many words to say in a day than the male does. Now a male who has learned this principle will also realize that God did this for a purpose. One fourth of the words that she has to get out deal with how she feels. One fourth of the words that she has to get out deal with what she's thinking. One fourth of the words that she has to get out deal with what she wants done. The remaining one fourth of her words is to explain to the male what she's feeling, thinking, and wants done.

It turns out that a lot of the fighting tension between men and women is over this issue. We were told that the husband was to live with his wife in understanding. This is one of those understandings that most men have not been trained in. The understanding is this, in a disagreement the wife may present her unhappiness as being an emotional unhappiness while the issue may stem from something she is thinking about or something she wants done. In other words what she presents as the problem and the cause of the problem may have roots in a different place. Any husband who is living with the wife in understanding will be able to root out the real cause of the unhappiness.

A scientific study showed that for the well-being of the wife, she needs approval of her emotions, her thoughts, and/or her actions. For her to be a healthy woman and wife she needs to have these approvals. It has been found that she needs on a daily basis at least 43 approvals. This is what a husband living with his wife in understanding needs to grasp.

The same study shows that for the well-being of the husband, he needs one truthful approval per day. When it comes to receiving this approval there is a mechanism involved with sometimes causes problems. This mechanism is basically that the Bible has stated and science has shown to agree that the female responds to stimuli. It is due to this response mechanism that it is hard for the wife to give this approval. This is why the Bible also tells the husband to live with the wife and not be bitter against her for something she may say or do. She responds to that bitterness and has no capability of giving him approval.

Having looked at the physical structure and the different needs of men and women, we now understand what God is saying in the Bible with a clearer sharper focus.

Return to the mystery (Understanding)

Let us review the mystery machine that we have created and fine-tune it. Let us look at the tires and axles, let us look at the grease God has supplied, let us look at the steering wheel, and then let us look at the motor with a finer understanding of what it means when God says the male and female shall become one flesh.

Colossians 3:18-19 (18) <u>Wives</u>, submit to your own husbands, as is fitting in the Lord.

(19) <u>Husbands</u>, love your wives, and be not bitter against them.

Ephesians 5:22-29 (22) Wives, submit to your own husbands, as to the Lord.

(23) For the husband is head of the wife, as also Christ is the head of the church; and He is the saviour of the body.

(24) Therefore, just as the church is subject to Christ, so let the wives be to their own husbands in everything.

(25) Husbands, love your wives, even as Christ also loved the church, and gave Himself for it.

(26) That he might sanctify and cleanse it with the washing of water by the word.

(27) That He might present it to Himself a glorious church, not having spot, or wrinkle, or any such thing; but that it should be holy and without blemish.

(28) So ought men to love their wives as their own bodies. He that loveth of his wife loveth himself.

(29) For no man ever yet hated his own flesh but nourishes and cherishes it, even as the Lord the church.

First Peter 3:1-7 (1-2) Wives, likewise, be submissive to your own husbands, that even if some do not obey the word, they, without a word, may be won by the consul of their wives, when they observed your chaste conduct accompanied by fear.

(3-4) Do not let your adornment be merely out word- arranging they are, wearing gold, or putting on apparel- rather the hidden person of the heart, with the incorruptible of a gentle and quiet spirit, which is very precious in the sight of God.

(5-6) For in this manner, in former times, the holy women who trusted in God also adorned themselves, being submissive to their own husbands, as Sarah obeyed Abraham, calling him Lord, whose daughter's you are if you do good and are not afraid with any terror.

(7) Likewise, ye husbands, dwell with your wife according to knowledge, giving honor unto the wife, as unto the weaker vessel, and as being heirs together of the grace of life; that your prayers be not hindered.

First Corinthians 7:1-4 (1) Now concerning the things whereof ye wrote unto me: good for a man not to touch a woman.

(2) Nevertheless, to avoid fornication, let every man have his own wife, and that every woman have her own husband.

(3) Let the husband render to his wife the affection do her, and likewise also the wife to her husband.

(4) The wife does not have authority over her own body, but the husband does. And likewise the husband does not have authority over his own body, but the wife does.

Looking at the tires that we have on our mystery machine, we have the husband and the wife and male and female. We notice that primarily the wife is addressed first in the verses. The wife is told to submit to her husband has is fit in the Lord. The wife is told to submit to her husband as if she was submitting to the Lord. The wife should be submissive to her own husband that she may lead him to the Lord.

Why is she told to be submissive? Submission is a required action by sheer will on the part of the wife. There is one thing we notice in these verses, she is not told to love her husband. Even if the husband is not lovable, she is still supposed to be submissive. Because she responds to his stimuli, she may fall in and out of love frequently. She may not even respect him at certain times. Yet she is to at all times be submissive to her husband.

God specifies this submission specifically because He realizes that she will not have it in her to love him at all times. Being in submission a wife may bring her husband to God as Sarah brought Abraham to God. By not being in submission a wife may actually lead her husband away from God much as did Eve with Adam in the garden. Worldly churches get the idea of submission as being something that a wife is forced to do, where in God's view this is something a wife wants to do.

The other tire (the husband) is told to do the one thing that he does not know how to do physically, mentally, or emotionally. He is told to love his wife. Why do we say he does not know how to love his wife physically, mentally, or emotionally? Recall he was structured to only be able to do one of those three at a time, and even then he very seldom does any of them.

For him to 'love' is a required action, a required goal, a required direction that he must do. This is how the world has developed a way of keeping the man in confusion by simply asking the simple question do you love me? Due to the fact that this question requires a thought, an emotion, and an action; it puts the man in a position that the man finds it hard to function in. This is why the husband is required by God to focus his attention to loving his wife. Then he is also told to live with his wife without bitterness, with understanding, and with honor.

The verses also explain a way for a man to do this without running into the problem of having to do three things at the same time. The husband is told to do this by loving her as he loves himself. We are told that no man hates himself, so by loving himself and loving her as himself he gives her love outside the framework of having to deal with the action, the feeling, and the thought. It all becomes natural to him to love her if he loves her as he loves himself.

This leads to the axles where she is in the relationship responding to him and he is in the relationship trying to love her as he loves himself. This is why we are told that he is as a husband to render unto the wife due benevolence and likewise the wife due benevolence to the husband.

We notice that this word benevolence is a feminine noun. Having developed a little bit of the idea of what a feminine noun is, we now realize that this is the internal workings of this relationship, and has nothing to do with the physical part of this relationship. Even though the female requires at least 43 approvals per day and the male only requires one approval per day, it is equally hard for her to provide that one approval to him as it is for him to provide all the needed approvals to her.

At this point God has taken out of the equation of marriage all of the factors that the wife needs to give approval to her husband and she is told simply to submit. God has also taken out of the equation all of the factors that a man needs to love by simply saying to the man love her as yourself, not as you love yourself but as yourself.

God places these two together with the statement that the husband should leave his father and mother and cleave unto his wife. We notice that to cleave encompasses the concept of her being part of his body, of his bones, of his flesh, and he is to love her as he loves his own body, his bones, and his flesh. We found that when God said that the husband is head of the wife, that the word head is also a feminine noun. We now understand that her becoming a part of him so that he could love her means that as the head of the wife he encompasses her needs as being his needs.

This is in essence why God frowns on divorce because as far as God is concerned the two became one. And God frowns on anyone who separates the one. He makes the comment that the one who separates or divorces the other commits adultery and causes the other to commit adultery, and causes anyone who joins with either of these two to commit adultery.

The only reason for separation, given to Moses as a writ of divorcement for his people which even God did not condone, was fornication. Fornication could come in the form of anything that causes the separation of husband and wife by an outside force. Adultery is the cause of separation of husband and wife by an inside force.

To steer all of this in the right direction, God said you are to marry as one man and one woman as husband and wife. The only reason you are not to marry is that you may be required to remain single from birth (John the Baptist), or single by the dealings of men (Samuel), or single by a goal given to you by God (Paul).

We started this study of Christ and the church. So let us now look at Christ and the church based on what we now know of husband and wife.

The church is considered the bride of Christ. As such the wife is told to submit to her husband just as the church is to submit to Christ. There may be times when the wife doesn't love the husband but she is not told to love the husband. She is told to submit to the husband and give him due benevolence. Now in the case of the church, because of Christ's love it is easy for us to love Christ. Yet even in those times as Christians (the church) when we feel no love to Christ, we are still to submit.

Christ as our husband loved us (the church) as He loved Himself and gave Himself for us so that even when we knew Him not He still loved us. He has required of Himself to love us without bitterness and with understanding.

We now have a fuller understanding of Christ and the church, of husband and wife, of man and woman, of male and female; until the time that we sit in His presence and understand fully.

I pray that this study has given you a little insight into some of the concepts that God presented in marriage, cleaving unto one another, and Christ and the church.

The great mystery (Christ and the church)

God used the husband and wife to describe Christ and the church. We will look at Christ (the body of Christ) first. Second we will look at Christ (the blood of Christ). Third we will look at Christ (the head of the church). Last we will look at God's intentions for the church (Christ's believers).

The body of Christ on the physical level is the work of God's role in the structure use of the X chromosomes. The X chromosome contains 1200 to 1500 genes according to our study. God has the choice of two sets of genes to use in the creation of a female.

Genesis 6:3-8 (3) And the LORD said, My spirit shall not always strive with man, for that he also [is] flesh: yet his days shall be an hundred and twenty years.

(4) There were giants in the earth in those days; and also after that, when the sons of God came in unto the daughters of men, and they bare [children] to them, the same [became] mighty men which [were] of old, men of renown.

(5) And GOD saw that the wickedness of man [was] great in the earth, and [that] every imagination of the thoughts of his heart [was] only evil continually.

(6) And it repented the LORD that He had made man on the earth, and it grieved Him at His heart.

(7) And the LORD said, I will destroy man whom I have created from the face of the earth; both man, and beast, and the creeping thing, and the fowls of the air; for it repenteth me that I have made them. (8) But Noah found grace in the eyes of the LORD.

Due to the corruption of the X chromosomes by the 'sons of God' joining with the 'daughters of men' God looked at mankind as being only 'flesh' and no longer spirit (the breath of God in Adam). God determined to 'destroy' all 'flesh' including mankind. Yet in Noah God saw some form of the spirit which He gave to Adam.

To keep that spark of spirit alive He had Noah build a boat to save his family. From that point in history God used the factor of X-inactivation to remove those affected genes. When He needed to bring in better genes He incorporated the males and females who carried the wanted genes. God even tells us of some of these inclusions in stories, such as in the story of Ruth.

'In due time' He had the correct combination of genes formed for a body for the Word to dwell in here on Earth. Remember for a male only the female X chromosome is available for the construct of a male body. Christ's body was of a designed X chromosome.

In constructing a male there must be a Y chromosome.

Luke 1:30-38 (30) And the angel said unto her, Fear not, Mary: for ^a thou hast found favour with God.

(31) And, behold, thou shalt conceive in thy womb, and ^b bring forth a son, and shalt call his name JESUS.

(32) He shall be great, and shall be called the Son of the Highest: and the Lord God shall give unto Him the throne of His father David:

(33) And He shall reign over the house of Jacob for ever; and of His kingdom there shall be no end.

(34) Then said Mary unto the angel, How shall this be, seeing ^b I know not a man?

(35) And the angel answered and said unto her, The ^c Holy Spirit shall come upon thee, and the ^c power of the Highest shall overshadow thee: therefore also that holy thing which shall be born of thee ^c shall be called the Son of God.

(36) And, behold, thy cousin Elisabeth, she hath also conceived a son in her old age: and this is the sixth month with her, who was called barren.

(37) For with God nothing shall be impossible.

(38) And Mary said, Behold the handmaid of the Lord; be it unto me according to thy word. And the angel departed from her.

I have highlighted some key statements made by Mary and the angel. ^a Referring to the collecting the right X chromosome genes the angel tells Mary that she has 'found favour with God'. As for the Y chromosome we are told more.

^b Mary is told that she will 'bring forth a son'. She wanted to know how this was to occur by her words 'I know not a man'. We are not informed whether Mary understood the genetics used in the creation of males and females, but we do know that she knew that to have a child there had to be interaction with a man.

^c We are told where the Y chromosome was to come from. The Y chromosome comes from God, not just God but every aspect of God. The Holy Spirit would be the worker of the chromosome

making sure it performed as it was intended. The Father would be the provider and selector of the required Y chromosome genes. The Word would inhabit the body and be called the Son of God. This collaboration would give Christ the correct brain, feelings, and blood (the blood of God).

Only God's blood could be shed for the penalty of sins. This would have appeared to be impossible, but when God selects the required genetics nothing is impossible. This is what the angel tells Mary. God made man the head of the union of male and female just as he made Christ the head of the church. [Ephesians 5:23] For the husband is the head of the wife, even as Christ is the head of the church: and He is the saviour of the body.

Just as the woman was brought to the man at creation, the church was brought to Christ at the shedding of God's blood in Christ for the sin of the world. This great mystery throws light on God's rights given to man. One of His rights is the right of His existence in man, and the right of man's existence in God. Another of His rights is the right of His role in man, and the right of man's role in God. God gave these rights (His rights) to man at creation, in a spoken and written form he presented them to the Israelites, and in the physical form of Christ God manifested His rights. We will explore these rights further next.

SECTION 3
God's rights

The Lively Oracles:
The Ten Words:
The Five Principles:
The Five Rights:
The Two Levels:
Given to Man

Introduction

In the Old Testament scriptures we read:

Leviticus 19:18 ". . . Thou shalt love thy neighbor as thyself: I am the LORD."

Zechariah 8:16-17 "'These are the things that ye shall do; speak ye every man the truth to his neighbor; execute the judgment of truth and peace in your gates: and let none of you imagine evil in your hearts against his neighbor; and love no false oath; for all these that I hate,' says the LORD."

Donald Frith

In the New Testament scriptures we read:

Matthew 5:43-48 (43) "Ye have heard that it hath been said, Thou shalt love thy neighbor; and hate thine enemy.

(44-45) But I say unto you, Love your enemies, bless them that curse you, do good to them that hate you, and pray for them that spitefully use you, and persecute you; that you may be the children of your father which is in heaven: for He makes His sun to rise on the evil and the good; and sends rain on the just and the unjust.

(46) For if you love them which love you, what reward have you?

(47) Do not even the publicans the same?

(48) Be you therefore perfect, even as your Father in heaven is perfect."

Matthew 22:37-40 (37) "Jesus said to him, 'You shall love the LORD your God with all your heart, and with all your soul, and with all your mind.

(38) This is the first and great commandment.

(39) And the second like it, You shall love your neighbor as yourself.

(40) On these two commandments hang all the law and the prophets.'"

We are to love our neighbor just as much as we love ourselves. We are to love '*the LORD your God*' just as much as '*the LORD your God*' loves us.

In this era the conception of love has the tendency to descend into corruption. We utilize love to denote any situation where we desire something.

Is there a definition of love in the scriptures?

Romans 13:8-10 (8) "Owe no man any thing, but to love one another; for he that loves another has fulfilled the law.

(9) For this, You shall not commit adultery, You shall not kill, You shall not steal, You shall not bear false witness, You shall not covet; and if any other commandment, it is briefly comprehended in this saying, namely, Thou shalt love thy neighbor as thyself.

(10) Love works no ill to his neighbor: therefore love the fulfilling of the law."

Galatians 5:14 "For all the law is fulfilled in one word, even this; Thou shalt love thy neighbor as thyself."

So the law and love are entwined as one word, ***"love thy neighbor as you love yourself"***. Could it be that the law presents us a clue into how to love?

[James 2:8] "If ye fulfill the royal law according to the scriptures, Thou shalt love thy neighbor as thyself; ye do well."

Is there more to the commandment of love than just our interpretation? Is there a perception of love to which we are to be aware? Does scriptural love have rules? Is there a plan for love of one's neighbor?

Let us look at the law which we designate the Ten Commandments for an outline of what may be scriptural love.

The lively oracles

^{Act 7:38} "This is he (Moses), that was <u>in the church</u> in the wilderness with the angel which spoke to him in the mount Sinai, and with our fathers; who received <u>the lively oracles</u> to give to us;"

^{Exodus 32:16} "And the tablets the work of God, and the writing the writing of God, graven upon the tablets."

Moses accepted for the church (in the church) fundamentals (the lively oracles) presented to him on mount Sinai.

What was presented to Moses? Typically the response given is the 'ten commandments' on stone tables. We get this idea via movies, exhibits, presentations, or interpretations communicated as fact from one person to another. What was presented to Moses on the mount for the church?

First let us look at the definition of terms involved in this presentation.

Let us deal with the word commandment. The word commandment can be used for words or oracles. Could this denote that these tables consist of ten words, statements, principles, or oracles? These words are interchangeable but for discussion let's use principles rather than commandments to arrive at a better understanding.

Why not call them commandments? A commandment in essence contains a blessing for fulfilling the commandment and a punishment for not fulfilling the commandment. Using this meaning of a commandment, it can be said that there is only one which could qualify as a commandment, and it is primarily ignored. Let us consider the one possibility.

^{Exodus 20:12} "Honor your father and your mother, that your days may be long upon the land which the LORD your God gives you."

Even though a blessing is applied (***days may be long on the land***), there is no punishment expressed for dishonor. The negative of the blessing is commonly presumed to be the punishment (days may be short). Yet nowadays this blessing appears to have no real significance in society.

Beside the blessing and presumed punishment, the image of how to dishonor your father and your mother is not represented. So how does one honor or dishonor? Could this oracle be ignored as not being a viable commandment?

Let's consider another example where blessings and punishments are not given.

Exodus 20:8-11 (8) "Remember the seventh day to keep it holy.

(9) Six days labor and do all your work.

(10) But the seventh day is the day of the LORD your God, you not do any work.

(11) You, nor son, nor daughter, nor manservant, nor maidservant, nor cattle, nor stranger within your gates.

Six days the LORD made heaven and earth, and the sea, and all in them, and rested the seventh day. The LORD blessed the seventh day and hollowed it. What is the blessing or the punishment? This has been superseded with man's idea of how to keep the seventh day holy.

The <u>one</u> oracle which by definition could be considered a commandment is:

Exodus 20:3-6 (3) "You shall have no other gods before me.

(4) You shall not make to you any graven image, or any likeness that in heaven above, or that in earth beneath, or that in the water under the earth.

(5-6) You shall not bow down yourself to them, nor serve them. I the LORD your God [am] a jealous God visiting the iniquity of the fathers upon the children to the third and fourth [generations] of them that hate Me, But showing mercy to thousands of them that love Me, and keep My commandments" (principles).

The punishment extends through three to four generations for a hatred of God, and all that implies. The blessing is of mercy for one who loves God, and all that implies. There is a deficiency in understanding what is implied. So the commandment is totally disregarded today.

Since only one of the ten principles appears to have true commandment blessing and punishment, then how could the principles be labeled as the lively oracles?

As the church who received these oracles, we want to consider what the principles signify in our life today. Being designated the lively oracles indicates that they have a life or value for life in the church.

So what do the ten principles mean to me? To settle on an answer to that question, there may be some other questions to answer.

Why stone tablets?

One question we could raise, Why stone tablets? We could avoid the question by seizing the logical answer, the scriptures says they were stone tablets. Another logical answer could be because Moses was on the mount and the mount was made of stone.

God was in the pillar of fire at night and the cloud by day. Could he not have blazed the principles in the sky like a neon light? Or write it as a special formation of cloud appearing as needed.

God created the rainbow after the flood. Could he not have embossed the rainbow with the principles?

God wrote with his finger on a wall for Daniel to interpret. Could he not have written the principles on the sides of the ark after it was created? Or even have them incorporated into the construction of the ark?

God spoke out of heaven when John baptized Jesus. Could he not have just spoken the principles when needed? Exodus 20:1 "And God spoke all these words saying, ..." He continues with the listing of the ten principles spoken to the people. So God spoke the principles to the people.

So why stone tablets?

Exodus 20:18-19 (18) "And all the people saw the thunderings, and the lightnings, and the noise of the trumpet, and the mountain smoking, and when the people saw they removed afar off. (19) And they said to Moses, Speak you with us, and we will hear; but let not God speak with us, lest we die."

It was the people who asked for Moses to talk with God instead of God talking to them.

If God wanted something permanent for the church, then tablets of stone may be practical.

God could have inscribed the principles on the face of the mount. Then the church would have a solid foundation established on the mount. As the church moved out from the mountain site, there could then be a returnable location where the writing on the mountain could be revisited.

Stone tablets are transportable. Being permanently transportable the tablets could be borne by the church where ever the church extended. Why then were the stone tablets placed in the ark, since the ark could not be touched without incurring death?

Why not set the stone tablets in a location for daily review? Today we can still see these principles on display in some public areas.

Why place the ark, with the stone tables inside, in the holy of holies where no one could enter but a priest once a year on a special day? And then God sat on the ark.

Could it be that the stone tablets were just a vehicle of transportation of the principles, and were laid in the ark so that the church would see that these principles were under the control or authority of God himself?

Had the tables been left out for display, could they be used as an image of the laws as done today, contrary to the second principle of no images of anything in heaven, earth under heaven, or the sea? Could it be that at the beginning of the thousand year reign of the messiah, when the temple is rebuilt that the tables will be the principles under which Christ will rule the nations? Could it be that they will be displayed then? Could this be why they are called the 'lively oracles' in the book of Acts?

Why two tablets?

Why two tablets? A typical answer would be that one deals with us and God, and one deals with us and others.

This concept would be valid if the principles realistically came in that type of grouping. However, there emerge only four which directly consider God, and six which consider others.

Was it because two tablets were easier for Moses to carry? How big were the tablets?

Exodus 32:15 "And Moses turned, and went down from the mount, and the two tables of testimony in his hand:"

Moses carried them in one hand. Was it because God could only write in a certain size letter and therefore needed two? Was it because God could only write on the front of the tablet and not on the back of the tablet?

Exodus 32:15 " .... the tables written on both their sides, on the one side and on the other they were written."

The tablets were written on front and back. Why five rather lengthy principles on one tablet, and five simple principles on the other? Do two tablets imply that there are two sets of principles being displayed? Do those two sets treat two different issues or classifications?

In looking at the first set of five principles; could there be a perception that these principles consider our relationship to God? As the principles are analyzed, these five could be designated the principles of us to our creators (include our parents, grandparents, and all those before us).

Then the other five principles are toward others? Would we not include as a part of the other our father and mother, or even God? What if these five principles are not about us and others but about us and our peers, those seen as being on the same level or plain of existence?

Why ten principles?

With all the principles for life which God communicated to Adam, Noah, Abraham, Moses, Job, David, Solomon, and others; why were these ten principles inscribed in stone? Is there something about these ten principles God desires 'the church' to grasp?

Since these were designated the 'lively oracles', there must be something about them which applies directly to our lives and existence today as much as it did in the past and will through the future.

We have five principles which impact our relationships with our creators, and five which impact our relationship with our peers. Is there a possibility that these lists are connected to each other? Could it be that the principles which communicate our relationships to those above us, and the principles towards our peers have any general analogy or meaning?

If laid side by side, does there emerge any common purpose in the two lists? At a glance, they would not appear to have any common meaning.

"The LORD your God which have brought you out of the land of Egypt, out of the house of bondage. No other gods before Me."	"You shall not kill"
"You shall not make to you any graven image, or any likeness that in heaven above, or that in earth beneath, or that in the water under the earth.	
You shall not bow down yourself to them, nor serve them.	
I the LORD your God a jealous God visiting the iniquity of the fathers upon the children to the third and fourth [generation] of them that hate me.	"You shall not commit adultery"
And showing mercy to thousands of them that love Me, and keep My commandments."	

"You shall not take the name of the LORD your God in vain, for the LORD will not hold him guiltless that takes His name in vain."

"You shall not steal"

"Remember the seventh day to keep it holy.

Six days labor and do all your work.

But the seventh day is the day of the LORD your God, you shall not do any work. You, nor son, nor daughter, nor manservant, nor maidservant, nor cattle, nor stranger within your gates.

"You shall not bear false witness against your neighbor"

Six days the LORD made heaven and earth, and the sea, and all in them, and rested the seventh day.

Wherefore the LORD blessed the seventh day and hollowed it."

"Honor your father and your mother, that your days may be long upon the land which the LORD your God gives you."

"You shall not covet your neighbor's house, you shall not covet you neighbor's wife, nor his manservant, nor his maidservant, nor his ox, nor his ass, nor anything that your neighbor's."

Let us look at the two listings three ways.

1. One principle at a time
2. Conflicts of principles
3. God to us and us to our peers.

Principle one - existence

Of the principles the first principle of our Creator to us would be the most unlikely of any type of a commandment. If the stones were a book, this principle would be like the introduction about the author located on the back of the book cover. What could the principle 'The LORD your God which have brought you out of the land of Egypt, out of the house of bondage. You shall no other gods before Me.' have in reference with the principle 'You shall not kill'?

Let us take a little side trip to explore who was the Author, and how did He address His principles? He starts out with the name 'the LORD'. Throughout the scriptures the name 'LORD' is an expression of His actual name. Names are labels of the personalities of the one who carries that name. So what characteristics of the name 'the LORD' do apply to the Author of these principles? The term used as an adjective such as an English Lord; references a master, ruler, owner, leader, authority, etc.

Could 'the LORD' apply to the Author as the one who established the principles, and will sustain or support those principles as the 'lively oracles' for life? If so, then these principles are not only what is expected by the Author of us, but is also how the Author handles Himself to the reader.

Where 'the LORD' implies a name of the Author and His authority over these principles; 'your God' implies that the Author has a more intimate relationship to the reader. God is a term more than a name and applies to actions, and the term god is commonly used as creator, originator, designer, etc. So the Author 'the LORD your God' informs the reader that He is the authority of their creation, their originator, their designer. This principle leaves no question as to Who was giving these principles.

The Author exists according to His own principles, rules, or rights. He expects us to accept His right of existence. How does this apply to 'not kill'? The concept of to kill is defined by the world as the shedding of blood and the taking of life. This statement deals with a physical action causing a death.

The problem is that more than physical death could be involved. What about the crushing of a person's spirit? What about the shattering of a person's ego? What about the destroying of a person's mind? What about the wrecking of a person's social standings?

What motivates one person to ruin another's existence; whether this is the body, ego, mind, spirit, social standing, or other quality the person holds precious?

To destroy another, the one being destroyed has no value to the one doing the destroying. Examples could extend from Hitler to the gossip (whether true or false) over the neighborhood fence. Merely because a gossip may be true does not indicate that damage is not being done in the transmitting of the gossip.

This principle is to understand that the other person has the right to exist. 'The LORD your God' has the right to exist. Your peer also has the same right to exist. This boundary must be understood. In the flesh a characteristic flaw of this principle can lead to emotional anger and physical assault when another person exercises their right to exist. This can be watched in children. Children are born with the sense that only they exist and all things are for their own needs. As they develop and encounter another's right to exist, this may lead to the hitting, screaming, tantrums, fights, etc. which they may display.

Just as you are to recognize the right of others to exist, your right to exist should be recognized by 'the LORD your God' and by your peers. To picture this right to exist of God, you and the others:

LORD your God	
Right to exist	
Right to exist	Right to exist
You	Peers

This right of God to exist does not clash directly with our right to exist given to us by God. In most cases the world does not care if God exists. Even part of those who claim to be of the church body function as if they do not care that God exists. Most have relegated God to be somewhere out there in the universe, and having no reality to their daily existence.

Our right to exist does not directly clash with our peer's right to exist. Most of our peers we do not even know exist, nor do they know that we exist. We act as if we prefer it that way. So the right to exist has no meaning to most until another right clashes against it, thus the words 'you shall not kill'. God's first and original right is existence.

Principle two – relationship

Principle two is where 'the LORD your God' wrote 'you shall have no other gods before me. You shall not make to you any graven images, or any likeness that is in heaven above, or that in earth beneath, or that in the water under the earth. You shall not bow down yourself to them, nor serve them.'

He also wrote, I the LORD your God am a jealous God visiting the <u>iniquity</u> of the fathers upon the children to the third and fourth generation of <u>them that hate Me</u>. I will <u>show mercy</u> to thousands of <u>them that love Me</u>, and keep My commandments.

What would the constructing of an image or likeness have in common with you shall not commit adultery? What is adultery? When, where, and how does adultery happen?

The definition of adultery today has been restricted to the relationship of marriage. This is one of a married couple having an affair with someone outside the marriage. Such a relationship could be physical, intellectual, emotional, congenial, sociable, or any other, where one is in a detailed arrangement with another over a common event. By extending that view, the idea of adultery becomes any act where one of the partners in that relationship brings into that relationship something which does not belong. Usually the introduction of an unwanted item into a relationship leads to the destruction of that relationship. Why? Unless both participants of the relationship welcome in conjunction the insertion of something new to the relationship, there is division.

To relate that concept to the relationship to 'the LORD your God', we are informed that He is a jealous God. He holds our relationship with Him in such a high regard that He is jealous of anything brought into that relationship which does not belong. Holding that relationship to such a virtue, He declares that He will consider us the same as one who hates Him, and He will deal with our children to the fourth generation as retaining the same corrupted relationship.

'The LORD your God' wrote that no other gods should be put before Him. No other item whether image (material) or likeness (intellectual) should be brought into one's relationship with Him. He calls anything introduced as another god.

What we have is 'the LORD your God' requires a pure relationship. Likewise 'you shall not commit adultery' means that in all relationships with our peers should be kept just as pure. Just as others have a right from you to pure relationships, you have the right to have others keep their relationships with you pure.

To picture this right to a pure relationship of you to the other:

LORD your God			
Right to exist			
Right to pure relationship			
Right to pure relationship		Right to pure relationship	
Right to exist		Right to exist	
You			Peers

God gives to us this right to a pure relationship, and expects from us a pure relationship. We can see this principle in Adam hiding after the eating of the fruit from the tree of the knowledge of good and evil. We are told that God came in the cool of the evening to walk with Adam and Eve as he always did before; however, Adam and Eve had introduced into that relationship something which did not belong.

God's right to a pure relationship and our God given right to a pure relationship with Him does not directly clash. Just as apparent in our right to a pure relationship with our peers and their right to a pure relationship from us do not directly clash.

God's right based on his existence is a right of his relationships to be pure.

Principle three – value

Let us examine the next principle level, 'You shall not take the name of the LORD your God <u>in vain,</u> for the LORD will <u>not hold him guiltless </u>that takes His name in vain' and 'You shall not steal'.

How would taking 'the LORD's name in <u>'vain'</u> relate to stealing? Could there be more to the concept of stealing than just the taking of someone else's property? Could there be more to the understanding of the term vain?

By looking at stealing as the taking of property from someone else, questions occur. Why take anything from another? Why not just ask, or buy it from the other? Why steal?

The assumption is that the other person would not give it or sell it because it must have value to them. If the other person gives it or sells it then the value is diminished in the world's system of values. Value is not the only reason for stealing. We give value to some things which no one else would give value.

What then is done with the item stolen? Three options are indicated;

1. To be sold,
2. To be used, or
3. To be destroyed.

Each of these options deals with the appropriation of the stolen property for wrongful use. Can more than material property be appropriated? There are musical propriety rights, intellectual copy rights, and workmanship rights, just to name a few. This implies that beside material values there are other more direct values which can be and are stolen. So the purpose of stealing is to appropriate the value of another with the intent of increasing one's own value. But by stealing, the value of the property is always reduced.

Let us investigate the term 'vain'. The term can refer to the diminishing in value by improper use. Then the image is that by use of the name of 'the LORD your God' by trivial use diminishes the value of His name. 'Vain' may be regarded as cursing or swearing. Moreover, 'vain' has the additional sense of using the worth of 'the LORD your God's name for your own purpose in a senseless application, thereby diminishing its value to Him and to others. He who utilizes the name of 'the LORD your God' for his own purpose, diminishing the value of His name, will not be held guiltless.

The use of the name of 'the LORD your God', even in basic communication with others which does not bring glory to Him, is using the name of 'the LORD your God' in 'vain', because the name is diminished.

The principle of the right of value (physical, mental, spiritual, etc.) to us, and the right of value we are to give to our peers builds on the previous rights presented. We have the right of existence and the right of a pure relationship; we also have the right of value. Just as valuable as God is to us, we are just as valuable to God. Likewise, just as valuable as we are to God, our peers should be just as valuable to us.

Principle three is the principle of honoring the values of others. You are not to steal for your use the values of the others, from material value all the way to and including the use of their name. Just as others have the right to have you honor their own values, you have the right to have your values honored by others.

To picture the honor of the right to value by you and others:

LORD your God
Right to exist
Right to pure relationship
Right to value

Right to value	Right to value
Right to pure relationship	Right to pure relationship
Right to exist	Right to exist
You	Peers

This principle of value comes into direct clash between God's value and our value, and our value and the value of our peers. God's right of existence and right of pure relationship gives God the greater right of value.

Principle four – truth

When listed side by side this principle appears not to have any general common foundation.

'You shall remember the seventh day to keep it holy. Labor for six days, but the seventh day being the day of the LORD your God, you do not work. You do not work, nor son, nor daughter, nor manservant, nor maidservant, nor cattle, nor stranger within your gates. The LORD took six days to make heaven and earth, and the sea, and all in them, and rested the seventh day, and blessed it and hollowed it.'

How does retaining the seventh day as holy relate to the principle 'You shall not bear false witness against your neighbors'? What is done on the seventh day? You are to do nothing which is done on the other six days. This is to physically display that the LORD rested on the seventh day. So in doing nothing which was done on the other six days as "the LORD your God" rested on the seventh day, we witness that it was He who created all things.

Genesis 2:2-3 (2) "And on the seventh day God ended His work which He had made; and He rested on the seventh day from all His work which He had made.

(3) And God blessed the seventh day and sanctified it (set it apart), because in it He had rested from all His work which God created and made."

As He created for six days, we work for six days. As He rested on the seventh day, we refrain from work as a witness to His truth. A false witness of "the LORD your God" is presented to the world by not keeping the seventh day holy (set apart) as He hollowed it.

We are not to bear a false witness against 'the LORD your God' just as we are not to bear a false witness against our neighbors. What false witness could we bear against our peer? When we say something about our peer or neighbor, did we actually observe what we are saying? If we did not actually see that which we are saying about our peer or neighbor then we are bearing a false witness. A false witness is a combination of truths, half truths, partial truths, or non truths. When you transmit gossip of your peer conveyed to you, you are bearing a false witness.

On a deeper level, what if you watched personally that which you are witnessing, is that a true witness? You watched what you were able to observe. But did you see the reasoning for what you beheld? Did you see the <u>thoughts</u> which generated what you saw? Did you see the <u>motivation or neediness</u> for the action seen? Did you see the <u>direction</u> of 'the LORD your God' in what you observed? Did you see all these, or did you see only what your eyes viewed? Was what you saw all there was to observe? As is often done, we only witness to what we think we see, missing all there is to see. In so doing we can miss the truth.

Now we have the basic principle, the principle of truth. Truth in what we witness of our peer. The witness of the truth of creation by 'the LORD your God' is in our keeping the seventh day holy. So, just as there is a right from you of truth from 'the LORD your God' and for your peer, you have the right of truth from others.

To picture the right of truth by you for others:

LORD your God
Right to exist
Right to pure relationship
Right to value
Right to truth

Right to truth	Right to truth
Right to value	Right to value
Right to pure relationship	Right to pure relationship
Right to exist	Right to exist
You	Peers

God has His right for truth from us, and gives to us the right to receive truth from Him. We are also to expect the truth from our peers just as they have the right to receive truth from us. God's existence produces His right to a pure relationship giving Him the right of value which requires the right to truth.

Principle five - role

'Honor your father and your mother, that your days may be long upon the land which the LORD your God gives you.'

Of all principles, the honor of father and mother and 'you shall not covet your neighbor's house, not cover your neighbor's wife, not his manservant, not his maidservant, not his ox, not his ass, not anything that is your neighbor's', would seem to be the most unrelated. Neither statement addresses an issue. Who dishonors their parents? Who wants their neighbor's goods? What causes dishonor of a parent? What causes coveting? What would I be trying to accomplish by coveting my neighbor's goods? We are not talking about taking their goods, which would be stealing.

In order to covet my neighbor's goods I must convince myself that to acquire my neighbor's goods I will acquire His role in life. If I had a house like his house, then I will be considered by others as they consider him. If I had a wife like his wife, then I will have a family like his family. If I had children and friends like his, then I will be loved and honored as him. If I had a job (ox) like his, then I will be as significant to others as him. If I had a car (ass) like his, then I will be regarded by others just as great as him. If I had everything like his, then I will be dealt with like him.

In having convinced myself that to have the same as him, what is it I am truly attempting to acquire? I must see and assume that his role in life is of a greater importance than my role, and I am trying to acquire that role.

The same principle applies to the honor of your mother and father. They are your parents and will always be your parents, that role cannot change. Even when the functions of care and support changes; the role of parent to child cannot, and will not change. The role of your parents will always be as your parents, you will never and can never be their parent. You will never create them. Even though the functions of care may change and require different requirements, the reality is that the roles will never change.

As a summary of the principle of role, we know that in relation to our parents we and they have a role which will never change. We know that no matter how much of our neighbor's goods we attempt to acquire, his role will always be restricted to who he is and not what he has. We have the principle of the right to one's role in life. Just as the other has a right from you to respect his life's role, we also have a right to our unique life's role.

To picture the right of the life role:

LORD your God
Right to exist
Right to pure relationship
Right to value
Right to truth
Right to a role

Right to a role	Right to a role
Right to truth	Right to truth
Right to value	Right to value
Right to pure relationship	Right to pure relationship
Right to exist	Right to exist
You	Peers

Because of God's existence and his right to exist God requires the right to a pure relationship with you. Because of his right to a pure relationship God requires the right to a value with you. Because of his right to a value God requires the right to truth from you. Because of his right to truth God requires the right to a role in your life.

Principles conflict

Let us assert that these principles are the rules which God uses to deal with us. They are the principles which we are to use in our dealings with others (God being included). They are the very rights which God displays and requires. Let us suggest that each of these principles addresses a faulty character trait in man. So what traits in man do these principles address?

We are commanded to love others as ourselves. How do we love ourselves? We set our boundaries by which we say this far and no further. For us to love others, we need to know the boundaries of the other. To cross those boundaries in love (as God loves us) we need to accept those boundaries. Even the <u>breaking down</u> of those boundaries by love, means those boundaries must be honored by us. In honoring their boundaries we build up those boundaries in the other. In building up the other's boundaries, we find that our own boundaries come into conflict.

Let us observe 'the LORD your God's boundaries as they concern us, and how they conflict with our boundaries. Then we will apply that process to our boundaries in conflict to the boundaries of our peers. There is a greater chance of conflict between the different principles.

The first principle is our right to exist. This right generally does not conflict with the other's right to exist. We both can exist, and not be in denial of the other's existence. The right to exist comes into direct conflict with the other's right to a unique role in our life. Without love this conflict can be displayed in some relationships of a wife with her mother-in-law.

The second principle is our right to a pure relationship. Our right of a pure relationship may have more of a chance of conflict with the other's right to a pure relationship than our right of existence to another's existence. Yet even then there is not much in conflict normally between our right to a pure relationship and the other's right of a pure relationship. The right to our pure relationship more likely comes into conflict with the other's right to our truth. Without love this principle can cause great problems in marriage circles.

The third principle of the right of values conflicts strongly in the world. Values come into direct opposition these days, and causes lost of society values. The right of our value conflicts with the other's right of value. Our conversations are comprised of value comparisons. Without love the conflict of values leads to other problems. An example of the value a worker holds of himself and his boss can conflict with the value a boss may hold of himself and the worker may lead to work related problems.

The fourth principle is our right to truth. The other's right to truth has little effect on our right to truth. We can determine if the other is trustworthy without the need for us to be trustworthy. This leads to truth being considered of insignificant value these days. Without love the lack of truth brings out dishonesty, lack of trust, unworthiness, dishonor, shame, disgrace, discredit, or disrepute.

The fifth principle is our right of a unique role in life. Seems there is not much of any conflict to our role in life and other's life role. The acquiring of a copy of the other's role in the world, especially in business, has become a normal part of social business functioning. The right of other's to exist develops conflicts with our right of role in life. The world to resolve this conflict creates ways for a person not to associate with others. Think about computers, vending machines, robots, touch tone systems, e-phones, wireless networks, web site buying, and other forms now created and used which require no association with any other person.

In using real love these boundaries and how they conflict with each other must be understood. Only then can the boundaries be crossed in love, and not have havoc. We will see the ways these rights can conflict, and then look at how God handles these rights.

Principle of existence verses role

LORD your God		
Right to exist		
Right to role		
Right to exist		Right to exist
You		Peers

'The LORD your God' created us with the right to exist, and we will exist forever. God says that he has a role in our existence. Just as you have the right to exist with God having a role in your existence, he also shows that he has a right to exist and you have a role in his existence.

A trait in man seeks to replace the existence of 'the LORD your God'. There would be no requirement to comprehend what is God's role in our existence. Then God does not have to be recognized. Conversely, by replacing God's right of existence, permits us to not be concerned with our role of life in God's existence.

We do the same with our peers. By destroying the others right to exist, we do not have to consider our role in the other's existence. Likewise, we do not want to recognize the role of the other in our existence.

How does this conflict function? Let us say that we have a detail about another which would result in the reduction of the other's status. When the other is around us seemingly pressing his role into our existence, our nature is to respond by circulating that detail. The world calls this gossip, something we use to release us of his being in our life.

With love the knowing of these boundaries admits a different view of their role in our life or our role in their life. Building up the boundary of their unique role allows them to cross the boundary we placed in our life. Our existence now has meaning in their unique role of life. Building up the boundary of their right to exist allows us to cross the boundary with the right of our unique role in their existence. Their existence now has meaning in our role of life.

The same applies to us and 'the LORD your God'. By building up that right of his role in our existence, allows the love of God to cross those boundaries. In the same manner the building up of the boundary of 'the LORD your God's right to exist, allows our love to cross as our unique role in God's existence.

From the very beginning of your existence God has had a purpose and plan for your life which He through love from time to time has reinforced or reminded us by using physical actions etc. By prayer we remind ourselves of the purpose and plan God gave us. The more you pray the closer these rights will blend.

Only by the use of God's love can this existence/role barrier be approached with our peers. When you acknowledge your peers right in your life and how it impacts your existence, you build up in their life their right to exist. As you build up their right to exist then they will be more accepting of the role God has placed for you in their life. If you do not build up their right to existence as you apply your right of a role in their life, you will be openly rebuffed. If you do not build up their right of a role as you apply your right of existence in their life you will be openly refused.

What is God's role in your existence?

John 1:3 All things were made through Him, ...

Isaiah 66:2 "For all those My hand has made, and all those exist." Says the LORD.

Revelation 4:11 You are worthy, O LORD, to receive glory and honor and power, for You created all things, and by Your will they exist and were created.

God's role in your life is your very existence. What is your role in God's existence? Your role is to honor and to walk with Him. Only through His love for you can you exist, and in a like concept your love for Him reveals His existence.

Principle of pure relationship verses truth

LORD your God		
Right to pure relationship		
Right to truth		
Right to pure relationship		Right to pure relationship
You		Peers

We can see a closer conflict of the principles of the right to truth and the right to pure relationship. 'The LORD your God' gives to us the right to a pure relationship with Him. By our recognizing that He is truth, all truth, and only truth allows His love to cross into our right of pure relationship.

Likewise, by giving the right of truth to God, we cross into 'the LORD your God's right to a pure relationship. Truth and truth only from us shows our love of 'the LORD your God' in a pure relationship and builds these boundaries.

Summarily, the same applies with our peers. The boundary of the other's right to truth is involved with our right to a pure relationship. When a peer becomes less trustworthy it destroys any purity of the relationship, and maybe the relationship entirely. Your untrustwortthiness crossing into the boundary of the other's right to a pure relationship destroys.

By love, knowing these boundaries and building them up, allows truth to build a pure relationship. Truth creates trust. Truth placed into any relationship builds trust and more truth. Most of the relationships in the world lacks the building up of these boundaries, and are destroyed. Truth has become a limited commodity. Trust has lost its existence in the world today.

Principles value verses value

LORD your God			
Right to value			
Right to value			
Right to value		Right to value	
You			Peers

The most visual conflict in character fault traits is the conflict of the right of your values to the right of the values of others. Herein we deal with ego. The value of each person is filtered through the ego. Also filtered through the ego is self esteem. The perception of value and the need for self esteem interplay in the ego.

Science has indicated that the conflict occurs when our value and self esteem comes in working contact with the other's values and self esteem. Before looking at that conflict, there appears to be an internal conflict in our own ego between our own values and our own self esteem. To the ego, values are the outside forces, much like an air pump to a tire which inflates but adds nothing to the essence of the tire. Outside values are needed to inflate the ego, but are not a true part of the building of the ego.

Self esteem is the internal value of the ego, which creates strength and structure to the ego. Self esteem is never created from outside values. This now becomes the conflict between our right to self esteem and the other's concept of our value. Like the tire, self esteem which builds the value of the ego (tire), may conflict with the outside pressure of the other's view of our value.

In this conflict we tend to look at our value of the other, not at the value they may hold for themselves. Their value can be deflated by the conceived value given by us. Similarly, our right of value can be pressured by the right of value of the other.

The trends these days is the notion that our ultimate value can be known only by the values given to us by others. We are inflated or deflated by the opinions of others. So our ego goes up or down based on how and when we are liked. We tend to look at 'the LORD your God' in the same framework of being up when He does something good in our life and down when He allows something bad to happen. We function by the pressure of others on our ego.

Self esteem comes more from knowing right and doing right regardless of all outside pressures. As self esteem builds up the value of the ego increases in strength and structure. The ego shrinks away from the need for outside values.

As it is with peers, the same is with 'the LORD your God' where He places internal values to build your self esteem, and not on His opinion of your worth.

Only by the building of the values of the other's self esteem in love, can the boundaries of the right of value allow your opinion to pump up the other's ego.

By their building of your self esteem in love, allows their opinion to pump up your ego.

'The LORD your God' works to improve your self esteem so that His opinion of you is understood. Your prayers allows your wishes and values to be considered by Him.

God and us

Keep in mind as we address the boundaries between God and us, God does not need for us to build up any of His boundaries. For our improvement, He wants us to function as if He does.

LORD your God
Right to exist
Right to a role
Right to pure relationship
Right to truth
Right to value
Right to value
Right to truth
Right to pure relationship
Right to a role
Right to exist
You

Let us now look at the conflicts without love of us and God. Then we will look at the companionship of us and God through love. We will look at the flow of principles from God to us, keeping in mind that the reverse flow of principles also holds true.

We claim the right to exist. Without love we saw in the world's view there is no right for God to be in our existence. The world says we have the right to be any type of person we want to be, because we exist and God did not make us. Yet it is by Him and through Him we exist and continue to exist. Through God's love we realize the right of God to have a role in our existence. By God's building up of our right to exist, His role is to improve our existence now and forever.

Building on the right to exist, we have a right to a pure relationship. God has the right to truth. Without love we find that truth is harder to identify from falsehood. The world comes to identify truth as anything which it wants to be true. We tend to accept anything which may sound good about God as being good and therefore truth. In love we are given God's truth to build up our right to a pure relationship. Since He is the Truth and the only Truth, His love keeps our sins from destroying our relationship with Him.

Because God is love, He will not destroy your value, but will increase your value (self esteem).

Without love we tend to think that we can have any relationship with God in any fashion we so desire and may find ourselves lying to God. Through love His truth in our relationship keeps the relationship pure. So too the right of a pure relationship with God requires only truth in all its forms and functions from us.

The world has attempted to prove that there is no God. God has been replaced with all manner of concepts to erase the role we have if God existed. Without God, we can be as God, and know good and evil as we describe good and evil. Every man becomes his own god, as it was before the flood. With the love of God, acknowledging the existence of God gives us a unique role of existence.

God does not need to have His boundaries increased. By love He allows the increase of our boundaries to increase His boundaries. His love crosses those boundaries to show to us how we are to cross those boundaries in love to Him and our peers. This is how to love your neighbor as yourself.

Donald Frith

Us and peers

Now to apply God's love to our peers, we will address the boundaries of us to the boundaries of our peers. The only way to cross a boundary is the building up of that boundary.

You			Peers
	Right to exist	Right to a role	
	Right to pure relationship	Right to truth	
	Right to value	Right to value	
	Right to truth	Right to pure relationship	
	Right to a role	Right to exist	

All your peers have a right to exist. Without love this boundary is crossed with evil results, even if the motive is pure or correct. Without love the boundary is torn down, not built up, or even recognized to exist. Hitler carried to the extreme the crossing of this boundary without love. The talking about what someone did to others is done to break down the boundary. Your ignoring, abandoning, abusing, or doing anything to a peer which indicates that the peer does not have a right to exist is done to break down the boundary. Yet any attempt to cross this boundary only causes the peer internally to build up their right to exist into a stronger impassable boundary.

With love recognizing the right of your peer to exist builds up that boundary. It makes your role in their existence more important. The building up of the boundary allows for a closer association of the next principle, the boundary of their right to a pure relationship.

With the other's right to exist comes their right to a pure relationship. Without love this boundary can be crossed resulting in separation. A father having incest with his child under the concept of love causes a separation between the father and child. Without love the telling of a lie to a coworker can cause separation between workers. By attempting to break down the other's boundary, the boundary becomes stronger and impassible.

Building up in love the other's right to a pure relationship creates a bond of trust. Knowing in love that only truth can build up the

72

boundary, then only truth is placed into the relationship. This allows a closer relationship for the boundary of values.

With the other's right to exist and right to pure relationships, comes their right to value.

Without love, their value becomes only the impressions of others, and the ego must be pumped by others. The boundary of the other's value is built up and torn down constantly until something breaks. Mental illness can be caused by a break in the ego through the inflation and deflation of peer pressure. When a mother constantly tells a child only how bad he is for having said or done something, can break the value boundary. Just like the other boundaries, the more the outside pressure the more the ego presses back. Egos can be created or destroyed by the worth shown by others. In love building up of the boundary of the value of self esteem reduces the need for peer approval. This allows for the level of the boundary of right to truth.

Built on your right of existence, right of a pure relationship, and right of a value, comes your right to truth. The other's right to truth can come in conflict with your right for a pure relationship. Without love the boundary of truth is crossed with deadly results. Death can come from the husband or wife who kills an unfaithful spouse in one extreme, to the person who tells their friend a truth in secret in the other extreme. The building up in love of your boundary of the right to truth creates a foundation for the right of a role.

Others have a right to a role in your existence. This right of a role cannot exist without love in the building up of the other's boundary of existence, pure relationship, value, and truth. With love it has to exist.

Given and broken

Let us look at where and how God's rights were given to man and where those rights were broken.

Genesis 1:26-27 (26) Then God said, "Let Us make man in Our image, according to Our likeness; let them have dominion over the fish of the sea, over the birds of the air, and over the cattle, over all the earth and over every creeping thing that creeps on the earth."

(27) So God created man in His image; in the image of God He created him, male and female He created them.

God said that He would make a creature called man, both masculine and feminine, in His image. This allowed man the role of ruler over all of earth's dominions. All which existed would look on man's existence as if they would look on God's existence.

We notice also that along with God making man in His own image, God also made man according to His own likeness. We notice that the creating of a man in His own character is for the domination of the earth and everything on it. What was the creation of man in his own likeness for? Could this be dealing with God's eternal rights given to man?

Genesis 2:7 And the Lord God formed man of the dust of the ground and breathed into his nostrils the breath of life and man became a living being.

We notice in this verse that we have no information about the domination of the earth. There was a uniqueness of breath given to man called the breath of life and man became a living being. If we were to look at the rights that God had, that existed with God; we would see that God had the right to exist in His creation, God had the right to a pure relationship in His creation, God had the right to a value in His creation, God had a right to truth in His creation, and God had a right to a role in His creation.

Before their fall we observe that Adam and Eve walked with God in the cool of the evening. God had an existence (principle 1) with His creation and they had a role in that creation (principle 5) given by Him. God had a pure relationship (principle 2) with His creation and they had truth for that relationship (principle 4) given by Him. God had a value (principle 3) in His creation and they also had a value (principle 3) given by Him. God had pure truth (principle

4) with His creation and they had a pure relationship (principle 2) with Him. God had a role (principle 5) in His creation and they had existence (principle 1) by Him and through Him.

^{Genesis 2:15-17} Then the Lord God took the man and put him in the Garden of Eden to attend and keep it. And the Lord God commanded a man, saying' "of every tree of the garden you may freely eat; but of the tree of the knowledge of good and evil you shall not eat, for in the day that you eat of it you shall surely die."

When they disobeyed God all of man's rights given by God changed.

^{Genesis 3:8} And they heard the sound of the LORD God walking in the garden in the cool of the day, and Adam and his wife hid themselves from the presence of the LORD God among the trees of the garden.

Man's role in God's creation changed from domination before man's fall, to subjugation to sin. Man stopped walking with God and instead hid from God. The role of man changed from God's original given role of domination of the earth, to the role of subjugation to the earth by having to toil just to survive.

^{Genesis 3:12-13} (12) Then the man said, "The woman whom You gave [to be] with me, she gave me of the tree, and I ate."

(13) And the LORD God said to the woman, "What [is] this you have done?" The woman said, "The serpent deceived me, and I ate." ...

Man's truth changed from pure truth to hidden truth and lies. Rather than giving the truth that he ate from the tree, Adam passed the blame on by blaming God for the woman which God gave him. Rather than giving the truth that she ate from the tree, Eve passed the blame to the serpent.

^{Genesis 2:25} And they were both naked, the man and his wife, and were not ashamed.

^{Genesis 3:9-11} (9) Then the LORD God called to Adam and said to him, "Where [are] you?"

(10) So he said, "I heard Your voice in the garden, and I was afraid because I was naked; and I hid myself."

(11) And He said, "Who told you that you [were] naked? Have you eaten from the tree of which I commanded you that you should not eat?"

Man's value that he had of himself and of God changed and diminished. Before disobedience they walked with God and were not ashamed. After the fall they were ashamed of being naked and were afraid to be seen by God.

^{Genesis 3:16-19} (16) To the woman He said: "I will greatly multiply your sorrow and your conception; In pain you shall bring forth children; Your desire [shall be] for your husband, And he shall rule over you."

(17) Then to Adam He said, "Because you have heeded the voice of your wife, and have eaten from the tree of which I commanded you, saying, 'You shall not eat of it': "Cursed [is] the ground for your sake; In toil you shall eat [of] it All the days of your life.

(18) Both thorns and thistles it shall bring forth for you, And you shall eat the herb of the field.

(19) In the sweat of your face you shall eat bread Till you return to the ground, For out of it you were taken; For dust you [are], And to dust you shall return."

Man's pure relationship with God, the creation, and each other changed from equality to being prohibited by God. Before their disobedience Adam and Eve were equal in their relationship with each other and God. When sin entered, God looked at His relationship to each of them individually.

Man's existence had been redefined by God as death. Before disobedience they would live with God in life. When sin entered, their existence was to live without God. God called this new existence death and cast them out of Eden.

These were man's rights given by God, perverted by disobedience, which Jesus brought back to man when He took on the form of a man. When anyone rejects Jesus they reject the rights given to them by God. The return of God's innate rights originally given to man is what Jesus did as he fulfilled the law!